BIG BLUE TRAIN

BIG BLUE TRAIN

POEMS BY
PAUL ZIMMER

The University of Arkansas Press
Fayetteville 1993

Designed by Gail Carter

The paper used in this publication meets the minimum requirements of the
American National Standard for Permanence of Paper for Printed Library
Materials Z39.48-1984. ♾

Zimmer, Paul.
    Big blue train : poems / by Paul Zimmer.
        p. cm.
    ISBN 1-55728-296-X. — ISBN 1-55728-297-8
    I. Title
  PS3576.I47B54   1993
  811'.54—dc20
                                                    93-23039
                                                      CIP

to Aaron Paul Zimmer
and Jelly Bean

A smart brakie keeps a firm grip on a grab iron or stanchion when he's riding the caboose platform. Inside, some roads have thoughtfully provided handrails running the full length of the hack. But the general rule is "sit down, brother," when the rumble of free slack comes surging down a mile of manifest.

Railroad Magazine, August 1949

Acknowledgments

Certain of these poems have appeared in the
following magazines, some in slightly altered forms.
The author and publisher wish to express their
grateful acknowledgments to:

Antaeus: "A Romance for the Wild Turkey"

Connecticut River Review: "The Weathers of Love"

Country Journal: "Indian Summer"

Crazyhorse: "Easter 1991," "What I Know about
Owls," "The Day I Became a Poet"

Cream City Review: "Lightning"

Denver Quarterly: "The Brain of the Spider"

Georgia Review: "But Bird"

Gettysburg Review: "The Existential Year," "Raw and
Absolute," "Remembering Power Hitters"

Heatherstone Poets Anniversary Edition:
"The Seed Bearers"

The Iowa Review: "Big Blue Train"

Laurel Review: "Omens in Southwest Wisconsin"

Licking River Review: "A Host"

Massachusetts Review: "The Persistence of
Fatherhood"

New England Review: "The Map," "A Rant against
Losses," "The Longing Season"

New Letters: "Intimations of Fatherhood, Operation
Desert Rock"

New Virginia Review: "Another Place"

Plum Review: "Despair"

Poetry Northwest: "Song of the Black Dog," "Shadows Flooding"

Prairie Schooner: "The Light"

The Southern Review: "Diz's Face," "Romance," "Aurora Borealis"

Three Rivers Poetry Journal: "The Beautiful Ethiopian Navy," "The Failings"

Yankee: "The Rainful Year"

"But Bird" appeared in *Pushcart Prize XVII, 1992*

"What I Know about Owls," "The Brain of the Spider," "Crazy with Love," and "Another Place" appeared in the *Breadloaf Anthology of Nature Poetry,* University of New England Press, 1993

Dedications

"Big Blue Train" to Clifford and Michele Krainik, who first provided the image of the train; "The Beautiful Ethiopian Navy" to John McGowan; "Crazy with Love" to Julian and Sylvia Wolff; "A Host" to John and Carol Wood; and "A Rant against Losses" to the memory of Tom Lloyd

Contents

Part III

Part IV

PART I

The Longing Season

We waken early to hear
A big blue train thrumming
In the gray distance,
Bedroom curtains billowing
As chill wind sweeps in.
I rise to shut the windows
Against change, return
To warm you in my arms.

Later we stroll in heavy jackets.
Insects are all down, bundled in webs
Under the last blood of trees,
Only most resolute birds remain,
Trees and bushes are thinned enough
So we can look deep into woods.

The longing season has come.
Winter like an old train, cold rust
And crusts of ice, runs on
A straight track to where we walk.

Fifty years ago, waiting with
My parents on a station platform,
I watched a soldier and a woman
Kiss goodbye. It was winter,
Their cheeks and noses raw,
But they glowed in their embrace.
I had never seen such urgency.

Now I reach for your mittened hand.
Under the headlong, frigid sky
I draw you near and hold you close.

The Persistence of Fatherhood

Yesterday the autumn finished.
I began raking it into piles
Around the house. Sue came out
And called from the distance.
I cupped my ears but could not hear
Through bare winds and branches rattling.

I thought she said,
"Your father's on the phone,"
And started walking toward
The house, until I remembered
He's been dead for five years.

Then last night this dream:
Suddenly leaves were children's clothing,
Blue jeans, caps and flannel shirts.
I raked them up, bent over by sadness,
Fatherhood all used up and gone,
Playthings and storytimes gone,
I swept and piled, doing my duties,
Only this caretaking left to do.

The Map

After the border was measured,
The pacing and sighting done,
We drew the signs and symbols,
Tiny oblongs of house and barn,
Tracks and roads that intertwined
Through fields and woods over streams,
Down easy rises, running
To places that seemed to matter.

Here we put hatchmarks of love, marriage,
Parenthood, Christmas and birthdays,
Dinner place and sleeping place,
The place where stories were told.

These tiny scribbles show where we saw
Sparrows twitching in gray snow,
Point to how fog rose from the river
And slid across abandoned meadows,
Snagging through sumac and prickly ash.

This is where bracken softened our eyes
And dawn wedged into the horizon,
Then here is where woods burned
And the river swamped its banks,
Rain snapping leaves aside,
Running its misery into our collars.

Here someone went on alone.
And there dusk began to obscure

Co-ordinates one-by-one
Until the map became a void
Silencing even the cornfields
That used to natter and sigh
All night long under the moon.

Crazy with Love

Crazy with love, the birds fold
Over each other and tie knots
Right in the middle of roads.
They sit around in greenery
Ogling and pecking each other,
Sweet-talking stridently;
Their titillation makes blossoms
In trees sprinkle and sing.

How can you keep good sense
With all this loop and flash,
Ponder serious career moves
Or forward knowledge
In some weighty manner
With this feather-brained high jinx
Swirling around your head?

It's enough to make you flap
Your sore, grinding arms
And blare like a ga-ga crow,
Crazy enough with love
To start some board-legged dance
And twirl until you tear a muscle.

Our Bodies

Another cold day in July,
The garden is in shock,
Bugs lie low and the fields
Are on hold. Birds fluff up
In the branches and wait.
Our bodies, puzzled
By unseasonable weather,
Corrupt around our spirits.

But tonight, though the corn is
Halfhearted in cold moonlight,
We see a young man dance
By himself to country music at
The Dairy Days celebration
In Soldiers' Grove, Wisconsin.
He holds nothing back,
Feeling his body so much he can't
Contain it, trying to jump out
Of his skin to start some newer,
More lyrical life. He sways, stomps,
Pumps elbows, knees stroking high,
Swings around, curling over
A ball of his own energy
As if trying to cover an explosion,
Giving us all at least some
Dim recollection of our bodies.

Fog in the Valley

Old combines dither and cough,
Cows amble vaguely into pastures,
Fences vibrate out to the end
Of their stringency, but all
This occurs beneath an opaque sea.

Last week in Manhattan a man
Walked up to me on a foggy morning
And asked for money. When I told
Him I had no change he exploded,
"Man, how do you think I *feel,*
Having to ask you for a hand out?"

The fog unloosens and slips
In patches up hillsides.
Hawks are first to ease off
Their perches, then small birds
Flitter out into the milky air.

Slowly things begin to connect,
School buses flicker along the berm,
Stitching together corners of fields
With houses, barns, patches of woods,
Things rise to take substance.

If I sold this house and land,
Took cash to the city and passed
Out hundred dollar bills all day
To destitute people, by evening
I could join them in the fog.

The Rainful Year

Year of storms in rows,
Lateral rain and sodden land,
Year of lightning and smoldering trees.
All summer the river runs tawny
And crosses its own loops.
Farmers watch their fields fill up,
Small fish wriggle into furrows.
The sun grows fuzzy with mildew,
Fog snugs in the valleys until noon.
Farmers snap at each other,
They stew in their pickups
And rut the boggy roads,
But all they can do is watch,
Wait for fields to tilt again,
And then the water in its
Own good time, will slowly
Return to its first intentions.

Shadows Flooding

While I grew dim and helpless
Before dozens of horrified strangers,
Four thousand miles from home
In that London breakfast room,
Back in Wisconsin animals were foraging,
Ready to be gone at slightest whiff
Of me, trying to live their year
Or two or three amidst the trees
In spite of me. But I was far away,
Strangling on a bite of toast,
My face magenta, turning away
To die the only way one can,
Surprised, alone with shadows flooding.

And in Wisconsin the bulbs
I had planted like little skulls
In the garden stirred and filled
With new ideas. Bugs unwrapped
And began to diagram the warmth.

But among teacups and tables
I was clutching at last light,
Saw the spectre leering at me from
The woods and was unable to hide.
Birds fretted upward in the branches
Until someone who knew my secret
Came behind and grasped me firm
And I could breathe again.

I blew out
And drew in that English morning
Down through the stems of my lungs,
Blew out and drew in until
Animals moved in the underbrush
And trees breathed with me again.

PART II

Teiresias:

At my seat of divination, where I sit
These many years to read the signs of heaven,
An unfamiliar sound came to my ears
Of birds in vicious combat, savage cries
In strange, outlandish language, and the whirr
Of flapping wings; from which I well could picture
The gruesome warfare of their deadly talons.

Sophocles, *Antigone*
Translated by E. F. Watling

Omens in Southwest Wisconsin

It was a time for slow-turning shadows
In the trifling of bird songs,
A swell of oats and clover,
Yellow moths feathered in rings,
Quivering on the sunlit paths.
On an afternoon like this
A man could feel too sure of himself.

Later, storms lined up and
Lightning laid about in the valley,
Not small, distant glimmerings of heat,
But lurking, savage bolts charged up
And searing when they came down,
Making my ears ring and skin jump.
It went on for hours this way,
Gashing trees in the south woods,
Running a ditch through the garden.

Then, almost in minutes,
The sky relaxed as if nothing
Had happened, the clouds pulled
Apart to blue and we could hear
The storms roll away toward Iowa
As tatters of mist slid off down
Grooves of the driftless hills.

But the rain had left a warning.
Spattering through the open study window,
It tried to wash these words away

Before I was finished with them.
I retrieved them just in time before
They slipped away into sodden paper
Like deer retreating into twilit woods.

Last night I dreamt of our house
Cut and polished by moonlight,
Tenderly secured by trees
And grasses. The stars were trying
To make it disappear by being so
Distant and measureless, but it held
Through rich, desperate seasons
And I woke to the myth of ownership.

This morning I walk the land,
Find constant reminders of
My evanescence—bones of old fences,
Strange, primal mounds in fields,
Foundations full of rusting metal,
Gray stumps and odd rocks in piles,
Brown and blue stone flakes
Washed up in the cornfield rows.
But most persistent of all,
In the deep woods broken trees
Rub slowly on each other,
Incanting strange, distant words
Which I do not understand.

What I Know about Owls

They can break the night like glass.
They can hear a tick turn over
In the fur of a mouse thirty acres away.
Their eyes contain a tincture of magic
So potent they see cells dividing in
The hearts of their terrified victims.
You cannot hear their dismaying who,
You cannot speak their fearsome name
Without ice clattering in your arteries.

But in daytime owls rest in blindness,
Their liquids no longer boiling.
There is a legend that if you are careful
And foolishly ambitious, you can approach
Them and stroke for luck and life
The feathers on their foreheads,
Risking always that later on some
Quiet night when you least expect it
The owl, remembering your transgression,
Will slice into your lamplight like a razor,
Bring you down splayed from your easy chair,
Your ribcage pierced, organs raked
From their nests, and your head slowly
Rolling down its bloody pipe into
The fierce acids of its stomach.

A Romance for the Wild Turkey

They are so cowardly and stupid
Indians would not eat them
For fear of assuming their qualities.

The wild turkey always stays close
To home, flapping up into trees
If alarmed, then falling out again.
When shot it explodes like a balloon
Full of blood. It bathes by grinding
Itself in coarse dirt, is incapable
Of passion or anger, knows only
Vague innocence and extreme caution,
Walking around in underbrush
Like a cantilevered question mark,
Retreating at the least hint of danger.

I hope when the wild turkey
Dreams at night it flies high up
In gladness under vast islands
Of mute starlight, its silhouette
Vivid in the full moon, guided always
By radiant configurations high
Over chittering fields of corn
And the trivial fires of men,
Never to land again nor be regarded
As fearful, stupid, and unsure.

Calendar with Deer

January
    bones under snow
    hollows in drifts

February
    hoofprints crossing
    an abandoned road

March
    flitter of snow
    whistle and snort

April
    bark slashed
    antlers in mud

May
    gaze   munch
    skitter of yearlings

June
    fauns suckle
    quiet   wait

July
    ferns   grass   herbs
    twigs   bark   shrubs

August
    corn   cherries   acorns
    apples   berries   plums

September
    moss scuffed
    cluster of scat

October
    muscle   grunt
    thrash   mount

November
    smears on pavement
    meat in truck beds

December
    new born Christ
    give them food
    keep them warm

A Host

It was as if a cherubim
had lost its fragile hold
and fallen out of a winter sky,
perhaps it was a grouse
that had flittered down
and landed for a moment
to leave its delicate
effect in fresh snow;
but in this time of
chill trees and bones,
of days strained slowly
through tense branches,
it is our only promise
to come to a place where
angels still can hint
of their existence
in newly fallen snow.

Song of the Black Dog

When my black dog sings,
Her eyes distant and longing,
She reaches high into her art,
Becoming light and air,
Throat held straight open and true
To the depth of her feeling.

Her sweet pitch, rising
To the far corners of the house
And out the window screens,
Moves the squirrels to thump
And scramble on the roof,
Scrolling themselves as they flit
Away through gossamer and twigs.

Her fine songs make big birds
Fan out of the meadow,
Whomping into air,
And little creatures scurry
To their brush piles.
Even the bones of a dead deer
In the south woods almost rise
In alarm to clatter away.

The Brain of the Spider

Imagine a spider's brain,
The various colored segments of its matter:
Crimson for power, blue for balance,
Green for judgement, yellow for cunning.
Think how it inspires the shape of dew,
How it squares frost and causes
The silver sweep of its filaments
To stroke your face in woods and streets.
Regard the air it fixes between strands,
Its careful allowances for time and space.
Then consider what is most complex:
The unnerving grayness of its patience,
White speed of its sudden charges,
The raven segment it maintains for death.

Threnody

With mindless resolve I toted the chainsaw
Downhill to drop some small trees
That blocked our view to the valley.
I started slashing their trunks,
Watching them shudder and topple
In slow arcs to the underbrush.

Insects gnawed my neck and arms.
By the time I reached the largest oak
Far at the end of the stand,
I was exhausted, raw and angry,
In weariness did not bother to notch
The trunk, but cut straight in until
The tree pinched down on the saw.

For a spell it held that way as I cursed
And yanked at the saw handle.
Then a slight breeze blew it forward
Just enough so I could snatch
The chain bar out. The tree leaned
Back again to close its grievous wound.

I dropped the saw into its dust
And wiped my brow. We stood
Together in the quiet, breathing hard,
Both of us stunned and exhausted.

Slowly the tree resigned,
Sensing mortal damage.

It made its final decision,
Gave up holding itself together,
Tilted and began to fall,
Turning and grinding on its injury.
Leaves in shock, branches shrieking,
It crashed into the underbrush.

Despair

January 1991

Always it is the same.
Ambassadors come home in despair.
We begin to stack the days
Like empty crates in a warehouse.
We speak the words of outrage.
Generals fix their gelid smiles for cameras.
This will be the fourth war of my life,
The same number my mother and father saw.

This morning I cursed a man
For honking his horn at me.
All summer insects rendered
And piled up chitinous corpses.
Once again it is our turn.
The air is frigid and raw.
A flock of crows rises,
Eating the silence above it.
We have come again to the cold
Weather of our anxiety.

Intimations of Fatherhood, Operation Desert Rock

January–May 1955

You trudge in shock across
the slain desert toward
the stem of the explosion.
Appalling fungus sprinkles
spores down on your helmet.
Everything you see is dead or suffering.

You were brought here
to be brave and mindless,
but some small thing bumps against
your boot—a baby jackrabbit
blinded and matted with blood.
You pick it up, feel it quiver twice
before it swoons in your hands.

Without thinking, in midst
of this blasted place, you undo
a pocket and gently slip
the rabbit child into the warmth,
then fasten the button again.
You hurry to catch up,
walk on with the others,
bearing your secret toward the fire.

PART III

Somewhere Years Ago

This morning long, corduroy clouds
Extend halfway up into the sky,
Rolling one after another like azure
Memories of the town woman
As she gives me her recollections
Of what had been lost to flood.

"First there was Schneider's grocery,
Next was Bolender's barber shop,
Then Doc Rubright's dentist office,
Then some tavern,
Then Ricker's hardware store.
There was eight feet of water in
Some places and the mud and stink!
I saw a rat riding a two-by-four,
Trying to stay alive in the swirl.

"Let's see,
Next there was Hoobler's drugstore,
Then McCrory's Five-and-Dime,
Then Richie's coffee shop,
Then there was Art's garage,
Then there was the Isaly's store.
Across the street at the end
Of the block, sitting in a little yard,
There was our house."

Somewhere years ago I read about
Sound waves rising forever into space.

If a person could get way out to
The right place beyond the dust,
They could listen to everything
Rolling up like a blue surf of sound,
All the things that ever happened—
Music and explosions, the fury
And gladness, cries of animals,
Bells tolling and drums beating,
Slow wind through tree stumps,
Factory whistles and cries of love,
Every hammer fall and rain splash.
All the great and small sounds.

But Bird

Some things you should forget,
But Bird was something to believe in.
Autumn '54, twenty, drafted,
Stationed near New York en route
To atomic tests in Nevada.
I taught myself to take
A train to Pennsylvania Station,
Walk up Seventh to 52d Street,
Looking for music and legends.
One night I found the one
I wanted. Bird.

Five months later no one was brave
When the numbers ran out.
All equal—privates and colonels—
Down on our knees in the slits
As the voice counted backward
In the dark turning to light.

But "Charlie Parker" it said
On the Birdland marquee,
And I dug for the cover charge,
Sat down in the cheap seats.
He slumped in from the kitchen,
Powder blue serge and suedes.
No jive Bird, he blew crisp and clean,
Bringing each face in the crowd
Gleaming to the bell of his horn.
No fluffing, no wavering,

But soaring like on my old
Verve waxes back in Ohio.

Months later, down in the sand,
The bones in our fingers were
Suddenly x-rayed by the flash.
We moaned together in light
That entered everything,
Tried to become the earth itself
As the shock rolled toward us.

But Bird. I sat through three sets,
Missed the last train out,
Had to bunk in a roach pad,
Sleep in my uniform, almost AWOL.
But Bird was giving it all away,
One of his last great gifts,
And I was there with my
Rosy cheeks and swan neck,
Looking for something to believe in.

When the trench caved in it felt
Like death, but we clawed out,
Walked beneath the roiling, brutal cloud
To see the flattened houses,
Sheep and pigs blasted,
Ravens and rabbits blind,
Scrabbling in the grit and yucca.

But Bird. Remember Bird.
Five months later he was dead,
While I was down on my knees,
Wretched with fear in
The cinders of the desert.

The Day I Became a Poet

A dead raccoon is splayed
At the edge of the cornfield,
Bloated, split open, reeking,
Brutal wounds on each side
Of its fractured neck where
An owl had dropped on it.

I turn it over with a stick.
Its sad, little belly the color
Of the last dingy ears of corn,
The color of Lester's moon face
That I recall from years ago
After Imbellis smashed it
With his fist, the blood
Suddenly out of the cheeks
And spouting from the nose
Onto the playground cinders.

Lester's vacant eyes turned
Inward on his pain, on a day
Long ago when light seemed
Filtered through tangled fur
And everything smelled like
Hell's wet ashes, and suddenly,
Standing in that ring of boys,
I did not want to grow up anymore.

Lightning

One night lightning slashed
The Orndorfs' apple tree.
From my bed in the little room
I watched it explode,
The flare igniting branches,
Blasting the ancient trunk,
A fountain of splinters blazing.

When the storm had passed
We rose from bed to survey
The damage. "Gone for sure,"
Old Orndorf said as he played
His flashlight sadly over
The naked, white shivers,
"Most likely a blessing,
It was blighted and old."

Now what am I to do fifty years
Later, remembering this when
The sky stops scrubbing itself
And pitches down to darkness?
Suddenly everything engorges
With driven water and air, thunder
Hammers at my body and lightning
Torches the veins in my eyes.

The Light

Warm evenings our house fills with light
And seeks breezes in its curtains.
I think of old, hot summer visits
With my uncle Joe, the miner from Indiana,
Blinking in his kitchen as he washed
A whole lightless day from his skin,
So weary he could barely change his shirt.
Yet when I begged he'd take his ball glove
Down from a peg in the closet and play catch,
Spinning a baseball with me in the alley
Until dinner, remembering tricks and
Fancy moves he'd learned pitching in
The Three-I League before his arm went sore
And they sent him home to the mines.

After dinner we'd rest with family
On the porch. Then Joe would rise
And beckon me to escort him
To the Moose Club. At the bar
His admirers tousled my hair
And set him up with round after round
Of Pabst as tribute to his best days.

One twilight as I followed him lurching
Home from the bar, a thin lid
Of ribbed clouds lit up and stretched
Across the sky past towers of cumulous.
As the sun slid away in a stripe

Of luminous pink, it silhouetted
The buildings of the little town.

Dazzled, I tried to detain him,
Wanting to share this glowing with him.
But he stopped only for a moment to gaze,
Then shuffled on through the dusk,
Wanting his bed, knowing that the numb
Moon spinning through clouds was all
The light he needed to find his way home.

Diz's Face

One of Diz's routines was to come on stage
And ask the crowd's indulgence while
His group tuned up. Then he'd stomp
The floor and everybody'd hit one crazy note.
"That's good enough for jazz," he'd say,
His great, wide face opening like a blossom
As he launched them into "Manteca."

Once in the 50s I went with friends
To hear his big band play a Cleveland club.
Between sets we spoke in awe of his flurries,
Powerful, cascading notes, amazing turns,
Notes perfectly formed, time locked in,
And the crazy, wriggle-hipped dancing.

Suddenly my friends looked past me in awe.
Tap-tap-tap-tap, on my shoulder—
When I turned there was Diz's face,
That marvelous, gleeful apple which could
Become a pear. He pointed down to my coat
Fallen from a chair to the floor,
Gave me a wink and went on to the bar.

Late last year he toured our town.
Before he played he cautioned,
"Y'all remember, I'm 75 years old."

Then his cheeks ripened and he
Dazzled us with a few strong licks.

Now here is his buoyant face in the paper.
Gone easily as he slept, it says.
In fifty years I've spent maybe thirty hours
In the same room with Dizzy Gillespie.
But here's my crazy, board-legged boogie
For him who once touched my shoulder.
Having no rights at all in this matter,
I'll presume to say anyway, by God,
Diz, that was good enough for jazz.

The Existential Year

I read the first three pages
  of the introduction to
    Being and Nothingness a dozen times.

I incessantly searched
  the streets for a woman
    who looked like Juliette Greco.

I learned to pronounce
  the word "Heidegger." I wore
    my coat on my shoulders

and long scarves which twisted
  agonizingly in the wind.
    I always looked

as if I were about
  to barf up my brains.
    I vowed I would never

look backward or forward,
  knowing that Being
    was enough In-itself.

Remembering Power Hitters

Donkey, Fat Pat, Round Ron, Swish,
Big Jawn, Pig, Klu, Moose, Tons,
Big guys who torched
The air with their swings,
But hoisted gloves as if they
Were front loaders and ran
Like herds of overfed bison.
When they fell down popcorn
Jumped out of boxes in the stands.
They were a million laughs
Until they finally connected.
Then we knew what they were there for,
Everyone standing up to watch
The numbers change as the ball
Went out like a goose in autumn
Over the upper deck light stands,
Over apartments across the street,
Over warehouses, rolling mills, bars,
Flying like the Holy Ghost
Over the Catholic grade schools,
Soaring above the slow freight
Headed for Moline, rising still
When it cleared city hall
And out midst sailboats
Bobbing in lake chops,
Never to be seen again.

Romance

This frightened, horny boy
Sits in a jazz club full of
Jungle ferns and leopard skins.

A piano trio is playing,
Dulcet and precise,
"My One and Only Love."

Hank Jones or Billy Taylor?
Al Haig? Ellis Larkins?
It does not matter.

What counts is this song
About something we do not even
Presume to hope for anymore.

Just in time, this wistful,
Tipsy boy hears about love
So sure it lasts a lifetime.

The Beautiful Ethiopian Navy

Having grown up far from the sea,
My friends didn't lightly heave-to
And go yo-ho-ho. They were men
Of the brush and distant peaks,
Young, reedy, black, intense,
They smoked unfiltered cigarettes
And drank straight rum.
Women turned to watch us pass,
Them in their crisp whites,
Me in my rumpled jacket and tie,
Negash, Maconan, Tassew, Seifu,
And Zimmer, like a rolling garden
Of dahlias and one elated lily.

Never have I had such friends again.
Brothers we declared ourselves,
Teaching songs to each other
And stories, how to throw spears
And footballs in Golden Gate Park,
Arguing games, books, religion
In the bars of San Francisco.

As I have remembered them,
Please do not tell me they are all
Likely gone, my beautiful fellows
From Asmara, Gonder, Harar, Diredawa,
Wandering parched lands of famine
And dying with the animals, or finished
In the bloody spray of politics.

Thirty years ago I watched them sail
Away to the other side of the world.
I have not had such friends again.

PART IV

Why didst thou promise such a beauteous day
And make me travel forth without my cloak,
To let base clouds o'ertake me in my way,
Hiding thy brav'ry in their rotten smoke?

Shakespeare, *Sonnet 34*

Raw and Absolute

Grinding his ropy cheeks,
A pitcher bends forward
And peers at the signal,
Bobs his blue-eyed head,
Then twists extravagantly
Into a broad windup.

But with his arms swung back,
The shadow from his cap dims
His forehead, and his uniform
Slips like a locust shell.

He hides the ball on the nest
Of his crescent paunch.
When he cocks his arm to throw
It is creaky and windblown.

He comes around as if half
Asleep, spittle stringing from
His open mouth. When he releases
He almost topples. The ball
Grows wings and flaps away.

When it comes back from
The catcher he rolls it
In his liver-spotted claw
And mumbles threats at it,
Pretending not to see the manager
Striding slowly toward the mound.

The Weathers of Love

Outdoors all day with you
In weather that cracks
Our small ear bones and drives
Rain through stones,
Snapping our coats like sails,
Suddenly in late afternoon
The scud is swallowed by blue.
Tiny flowers unwrap in sunlight,
Moss begins to passion.
So we have done it again,
Walked all day to love.

2.

Today there was light sifting
Of snow from a joyless sky,
No great burden, just something
For us to bear up under.
But tonight we can count on nothing.
The house begins cracking,
Big dogs moan on their rugs,
Pipes grow cold and indifferent,
Chill slips into our knuckles.
Twenty false steps outdoors
In the frigid, hard edges of air would
Shiver us, so we hold each other
And give the fire everything it needs.

3.

You swat a sunlit cabbage moth
With your white baseball cap,
Shouting and flinging organic dust.

The garden goes on contending
With itself, great heads wrap and tighten,
Vines quietly pump up their fruits,
Vegetables sit on their secrets.

Still you imagine perfection
And fear the gnawing worm.
I cheer you on,
Get that son of a bitch!
I fall in love some more.

4.

What to say to our children
Of our long time
In the weathers of love?

That it was never what we predicted,
But what we learned in time.

That to see you waving to me
From a hazy distance is as precious
As holding you in my arms.

That sometimes on a rainy day
Just knowing you are
In the next room saves my life.

Aurora Borealis

Years ago I felt spectacular in winter,
Worked the night shift in the open hearth,
Laboring for hours in a sweaty t-shirt.
Then at break I'd slip out into the millyard
And watch steam rise from my skin
As powdery snow swirled up into the stars.

One night northern lights stroked the sky,
And I became so dazzled I forgot the cold,
Almost perishing from exposure
Before I remembered that winter
Will take everything if you let it.

Today for hours I've drudged numbly in bare trees,
Thinning crowded woods, irritable as a porcupine,
Cheeks blazing, shoulders strained apart with pain,
Dragging firewood and brush uphill through drifts.

I work through dusk into the dark,
Then, in that silence look up to see
The vast spill of milky way and rays
Of northern lights sliding through
The stars—not just flickers on the horizon,
But long beacons reaching across the sky,
Folding and slipping over each other
Between shimmering patches
Of blue and rose-colored light.

For a while all this radiance and throbbing
Sets me back on my cold heels,
Holds me still among the branches.

But these days I do not forget the winter,
Feel it probing at my eyes and nostrils.
Ill wind thudding against my loins,
I throw the tools into the pickup,
Hit the starter and head for home.

Indian Summer

Out in the colors this morning
We found a grouse crumpled
Like a cottonwood leaf. Something
Heard us and ran away before it
Had a chance to clean the bones.

Last night a strident yipping
From the woods pricked into our sleep.
Coyotes come with Indian summer.
You hear them through the open windows
And remember their songs all winter.

Taken by warmth we forget the sleet
And hard air that sliced through our
Sweaters and jackets. Now in this brightness
The leaves begin to think twice.

But coldness creeps back on us,
Slinking up in dry grass
Through rough skeletons of flowers
Like a hunter on a foolish bird.

Northumbria

I followed the track of St. Cuthbert
Through his Celtic country of wind
And horizontal rain, saw where
He had healed the sick and loved
His flock thirteen centuries ago.
I witnessed how time and weather
Had worn his honored places.

I went as an American stranger,
Agnostic, no possible connection
Except remote and guilty longing.
I seemed to crave an antique faith,
But exploring in those dank,
Washed-out shrines and churches,
I felt little except the cold.

Then came at least a sad epiphany,
A thing that somehow assuaged me.
In a churchyard an ancient oak
Had been downed by recent gales,
Its fractures painful to behold.
All birds and small animals were
Dashed out of its snug, brown hollows.

Huge, benevolent, an irreplaceable god
Who had blessed us all for a thousand years,
Now had been cast down into weariness
And sweet relief like the rest of us
Amidst high wind and streaks of rain.

A Rant against Losses

Word has come of my friend's death in London.
In my desolation memories begin to roll.
I recall once looking for him in the pubs
When a young barman, pondering my inquiry,
Smirked, "Red nose and a pint of cider, right?
The knobby one who zigzags when he walks?"

I should have slammed his pearly teeth,
Stood him on his diapered head and shaken
The little drums from his ears! Even now
It soothes me to hope that his old age
Becomes tawdry, that his hair falls out,
That his joints ignite and ache incessantly.

For my friend was worn fine with civility,
A wise, endearing man, lover of words,
To be respected beyond the capacity
Of any modish, indifferent, callow wag.
God damn ridiculous, vacant youth,
And piss on you, death, and fuck you!

The Seed Bearers

I dream the Spring of 1901,
My grandfathers walk together in
Their shirt sleeves through woods,
Trailing smoke from their cigars.
The French and German man,
A miner and accountant,
Never met so far as I know,
But talking American,
They laugh and josh each other
Like colors plucked randomly
From light and clouds, nurtured
In dim pods, then bloomed forth
Arm-in-arm in the springtime.

Victoria has died, Bismarck and Verdi.
Hemingway, Ellington, Lorca are born.
We've fought a pitiless Civil War.
McKinley has been re-elected
And soon will be assassinated.
We have been rudely led for years,
Assaulted by our inventions,
But my grandfathers walk on,
Guileless and blossoming in America.

• • •

Now the century has almost passed.
We approach the double millenium.
My grandfathers are long dead,
But my son, his son, and I,

Still colors plucked from light
And clouds, stroll in the spring.
Many great people have died.
We do not know who has just
Been born. The vacant wars have
Gone on, a president gunned down,
Another resigned, we are spent out,
Have been cruelly led for years.
But this is what we can do,
Grandfather, father and son,
We blossom forth arm-in-arm
Through spring trees and grasses,
Burrs and seed fluff clinging
To our jeans and t-shirts, strolling,
Talking together in the last light
Of this old and failed century.

The Failings

1. Detachment

One spring morning I awoke imagining
All my visionary options still were open,
But then, swirling inside my left
Eyeball, came a black blizzard.

Detached retina, the doctor told me,
Reducing all my options to but three:
A slow withdrawal into darkness,
A buckle stitched around my eyeball,
Or a bubble inserted into my humor.
One unacceptable, two frightening,
I chose the third to gently nudge
My retina back into its place.

Now, despite its healing,
The drab inconstancy
Of my left eye becomes apparent.
It has declared its difference,
Denies kinship with the right,
Goes the way of dullness and self-pity.
I swear by the fresh gods of spring
That I will not follow its example.

2. Advice

At my age the only bird
I can hear is the crow.
Under these ponderous skies
I listen to him blaring
In distant fields and trees,
Giving his free advice to others.
He knows my problems, too.
He flies outside my window,
Yacking and fouling,
Drilling his uproar through
My hearing aids. He says,
More rain is coming.
Do not feel sorry. Stand up
And prepare yourself. There are
No excuses. No excuses.

3. Skin

Beginning as a perfect zero
Skin was inescapable memory.
It started sketching on itself
When at first it felt
The pain of air,
Making lists, assuming
Light of the sun
Or moon into its layers.

At length it abandoned purity,
Believed only in constant change,
Doubling and quadrupling
To become a semaphore:
Red for health, green for sickness,
Descending gray for anger,
A roily pink for love.

It spent decades shedding
And repairing itself. Now,
Anguished by its imperfection
And futility of its duties,
It moves again to flawless zero.

4. Body

Here is the old fool suddenly overrun,
Sitting on a slice of oak and breathing hard.
It's my body, overworked cutting wood,
Stomach burning, breath short, a cold wind
Blown up to knock the cap from its head.

I am tired of grieving for the failings
Of this thing that spends summer
In feeble recollection and winter
Trying to turn itself inside out.
Some days not even sun nor the tender,
Lingering descent of snow into its eyes
Can divert it from clinging wearily to its bones.

As I sit amidst its exhaustion,
I wish to see my body as it really is,
Not as democracy or tattered coat upon a stick,
Not as a heavy bear, not as rows of
Dingy curtains, nor a birdcage for my soul,
But as certain things beyond organs and frame:

Small centers of blind devotion to my being,
Bundles of pure desire and awesome fecundity
Still dutifully repairing and renewing all
My parts though doomed to failure.

Easter 1991

I tell you the wind in grooves and corners
Of this small cabin became plainsong voices
Drifting up, down, and folding through each
Other like flocks of birds over the fields,
A holy sign I was too numb to recognize.

St. John of the Cross wrote that souls
Suffer an agony of impatience to see God,
But after a new year of shameful war,
Our lies, slaughter and cruel posturing,
My soul was too full of self-loathing
And anguish for such hollow longing.

Through weather that had exhausted
The landscape with a whole year of
Conditions in one day, snow, rain,
Sun-warmed stillness to cold bluster,
I would have been incredulous or angry
If you or anyone else had tried
To tell me that a wispy cross would
Be mounted on a billow shelf of cloud
High in the last sun of Easter.

But now, despite risk of ridicule,
I must tell you it was so.
Looking from my window I saw it,
This least believable of apparitions,
Radiant for minutes amidst the contrails
Before folding over to become
A body tended by desolate mourners.

Another Place

You come to a place in winter woods
That seems remembered, a foundation
Full of rusty tools, door knobs, dog bones,
Peach stones, scissors, where hard winds
Blew for years through blackened timbers.
Small wings of frost still strive on weeds,
But so many things are missing now,
Pervasive regret has assumed the place.
You feel fine snow flitter down
And settle into the ancient residue,
Gathering in cockle burrs, ear holes,
Joints of aspen, sockets of your eyes.
Slowly it begins to change you
Into something better than yourself.

Big Blue Train

The big blue train coughs,
coughs again and is silent,
then resolves itself and slams
its pistons down once more.

They stroke three times, sighing
and blowing, then stagger cold.
Next time they bluster once,
hold the cycle and gather fire.

Fire on fire, and the engine
heats up glowing on the tracks.
It hisses, tensing its wheel rods,
impatient to connect its gears.

Clouds of steam and black smoke
billow up to the station canopy,
slip along the filthy girders
to curtain out to the sky.

Zimmer pulls the whistle chord
and cleaves the chill air in two.
Doors are slamming, signals flash,
people kiss on the concourse.

He taps the gritty meters,
eases slowly up on the brake
and brings the throttle down—
the engine knocks and heaves.

A long, echoing chain of thunder,
then the big blue train inches
forward out of the station,
creaking and swinging its lanterns,

slides into the early dawn,
through lighted grids of the city,
faces in its windows growing
vague in the rising light.